The Anthrobsce

The Anthrobscene

Jussi Parikka

University of Minnesota Press
Minneapolis

Published by the University of Minnesota Press, 2014
111 Third Avenue South, Suite 290
Minneapolis, MN 55401-2520
http://www.upress.umn.edu

The University of Minnesota is an equal-opportunity educator and employer.

Contents

Forerunners: Ideas First from the University of Minnesota Press

Original e-works to spark new scholarship

Forerunners is a thought-in-process series of breakthrough digital works. Written between fresh ideas and finished books, Forerunners draws on scholarly work initiated in notable blogs, social media, conference plenaries, journal articles, and the synergy of academic exchange. This is gray literature publishing: where intense thinking, change, and speculation take place in scholarship.

Jussi Parikka, *The Anthrobscene*

John Hartigan Jr., *Aesop's Anthropology: A Multispecies Approach*

Reinhold Martin, *Mediators: Aesthetics, Politics, and the City*

Introduction

They penetrated to the bowels of earth and dug up wealth, bad cause of all our ills.
—Ovid, *Metamorphoses*

This is an essay about not only the anthropocene but the anthr*obscene*. It responds to past years of discussions in media arts, cultural theory, and philosophy about the geological underpinnings of contemporary media culture. In short, the anthropocene has been the focus of intense debate and variation: finally, one felt, a concept to describe the effects of the human species and its scientific-technological desires on the planet. And yet it is a concept that also marks the various violations of environmental and human life in corporate practices and technological culture that are ensuring that there won't be much of humans in the future scene of life.

In any case, the notion of the anthropocene was preceded by notions of Gaia and even the nineteenth-century concept of the anthropozoic age. Antonio Stoppani stands as one of the early formulators of the idea that humans initiated a specific geological period. His 1870s visionary accounts painted a picture of the various strata of the earth. But for Stoppani, in *Corso di Geologia* (1873), such layers derived not only from earth's prehistory but were attributes of a planet unearthed by human technologies and then covered with the ruins of those inventions. The earth feeds that process and disappears under it:

> Rival of the potent agents of the internal world, man undoes what nature has done. Nature has worked for centuries at agglomerating in the bowels of the earth oxides and metallic salts; and man, tearing them out of the earth, reduces them to native metals in the heat of his furnaces. In vain you would look for a single atom of native iron in the earth: already its surface is enclosed, one could say, within a web of iron, while iron cities are born from man's yards and float on the sea. How much of the earth's surface by now disappears under the masses that man built as his abode, his pleasure and his defense, on plains, on hills, on the seashores and lakeshores, as on the highest peaks! By now the ancient earth disappears under the relics of man or of his industry. You can already count a series of strata, where you can read the history of human generations, as before you could read in the amassed bottom of the seas the history of ancient faunas.[1]

Stoppani imagines the future fossil layers of technological rubbish: paleontologies that deal not only with the earth but the earth after the appearance and effect of modern science and technology. His views express a curious theme of the nineteenth century, all the more relevant now. As John Durham Peters argues, the century of the sciences of geology and evolution theory, from Charles Lyell to Charles Darwin, was also relevant to how scientific thought implicitly perceived the earth as media. In these disciplines the earth was a sort of a recording device. The new discoverers of astronomy gradually perceived the cosmic dimensions of space and time in mediated ways. Such sciences were mediated by their instruments. In addition, geology and astronomy are, in Peters' words "always also media studies; they necessarily study not only the content, but signal and channel properties as well."[2] They allow us to imagine time-space relations far beyond what Harold A. Innis initially included as part of his pioneering media history.

In the context of recent media theory we are already aware of the work by Bruce Sterling (dead media, media turned paleontological) and Siegfried Zielinski (deep time of the media). The geophysical sphere features as an growing part of art festivals, such as recently at the transmediale Afterglow-festival (2014) in Berlin. Even entering the Haus der Kulturen der Welt conference venue opens a view of several pieces of survey equipment, reinstalled to function as peephole-style viewing devices—but not to the geological landscape: instead, they present media landscapes, measurement of online activities and processes. The Critical Infrastructure project by Jamie Allen and David Gauthier is emblematic of this drive toward geological and geophysical metaphors in media arts and technological discussions. In addition, it is complemented by the constantly growing interest in electronic waste and energy issues as well as larger questions of energy.[3] One can start reading history of media and technology before media becomes media. Even statistics about minerals tell this story: the increase since the 1990s in the consumption of indium, peaking in 2008; the growing numbers for import and consumption of silicon since the 1950s; a similar increase in consumption of rare earth minerals since the 1950s.[4] Of course, not all minerals are meant for media technologies—far from it (although media culture is the focus of this essay).

Whether or not they are perceived in terms of media, deep time resources of the earth are what makes technology happen. The emergence of geology as a discipline since the eighteenth and nineteenth centuries as well as the techniques of mining developed since then are essential for media-technological culture. Institutions such as the U.S. Geological Survey have gradually grown to be about much more than "just" geology: they are sites of transformation where the earth becomes an object of systematized knowledge and the knowledge thus created of the earth's resources is mobilized toward technological production, governmental geopolitics, and increasingly a global survey of the minerals of the earth.

Even if media theory might have *partly* forgotten the existence of the earth as a condition of media, the arts did not. In addition to the history of media derivable from the earth sciences, artistic practice from sculpture to painting to (for instance) the chemical worlds of photography has had a close relationship to earth's materials. Art has turned chemicals, clays, pigments into expressions of not only any romantic artistic spirit but the existence of the earth: an understanding of the earth's tendencies to create sound, light, and more.

This is one interesting way to understand the Deleuzian emphasis on the earth picked up by Elizabeth Grosz. The link between the earth and art is fundamentally conditioned by the existence of inorganic life: the fact that the earth is anyway, already, expressive in an ontological sense. The emergence of sexualized life on earth is one feature that carries forward the expressive qualities of matter. Grosz maps Gilles Deleuze's focus on the architectural as taking priority over the body, and makes the case that this territorial impulse defines our relation to the earth.[5] It's this architectural angle that feeds forward to architectures of the technological kind: computational architectures, planetary architectures of technology ("the stack" in Benjamin Bratton's coinage),[6] and other similar frames that take advantage of the inorganic life of the earth. This is not the full story. In the Deleuzian framework, further reworked into a creative feminist mix with Darwin, Grosz reminds us that art and the earth are producing in excess—not merely for functional ends and definitely not mainly for the convenient pleasure of technological corporatization of the planet as part of the further layer covering the soil.

Artist Robert Smithson spoke about "abstract geology," referring to how tectonics and geophysics pertain not only to the earth but also to the mind; abstract geology is a field where a geological perspective is distributed across the organic and inorganic division. Its reference to the "abstract" might attract those with a Deleuzian bent and resonate with the concept of "abstract machines." But Smithson's interest was in the materiality of the art practice, reintroducing metals (and hence geology) back to the studio. What's more, Smithson was ready to mobilize his notion, emerging in the artistic discourse of land art in the 1960s with a conceptualization of technology that we can say was nothing less than anti-McLuhanian: instead of seeing technology as extensions of mankind, technology is aggregated and "made of the raw materials of the earth."[7] From our twenty-first-century perspective, approximately fifty years after Smithson's practice, it starts an imaginary alternative media theoretical lineage that may not include McLuhan, Kittler, and their like, but instead writes a story of materials, metals, chemistry, and waste. These materials articulate the high-technical and low-paid culture of digitality. They also provide an alternative materialism for the geophysical media age.

*

This short essay works in the context of deep time. It discusses Zielinski's inspiring archaeology-related notion of media but insists that it become deeper and more material and reach to further time scales: millions of years of variantological media history. Hence I am using the notion of an *alternative* deep time. The text is a precursor to a longer project, a short of a teaser or trailer: it asks how to think about the underground in the age of resource depletion, a Cold War–style energy race, and the investment in the bottoms of the seas. It proposes the depths of mines as essential places for the emergence of technical media culture—from the entertainment sector to the military.

But why the anthrobscene? Why not just adapt to the normalized use of the anthropocene?[8] In short, the addition of the obscene is self-explanatory when one starts to consider the unsustainable, politically dubious, and ethically suspicious practices that maintain technological culture and its corporate networks. The relation of the mineral ore coltan, essential in cellphone manufacture, to the bloody civil war in Congo and the use of child labor has been discussed now for some years in cultural theory. In media arts, pieces such as *Tantalum Memorial* (2008, by Harwood, Wright, Yokokoji) represent projects relating to the mineral politics of media. We can remind ourselves of the environmentally disastrous consequences of planned obsolescence of electronic media, the energy costs of digital culture, and, for instance, the neocolonial arrangements of material and energy extraction across the globe. Jennifer Gabrys is one of the inspiring writers who have pointed out the need to start from the other side—the electronic waste and the accident—in order to grasp the full picture of media-cultural materiality.[9] To call it "anthrobscene" is just to emphasize what we knew but perhaps shied away from acting on: a horrific human-caused drive toward a sixth mass extinction of species.[10] To go underground is an analytical but also an ethico-esthetic choice. To investigate the geology of media is a theoretical contribution to the analysis of this situation of the anthrobscene. This essay is a preamble to a forthcoming book titled "A Geology of Media."

Much technopolitical vocabulary has emphasized other sorts of things. The immaterialization of digitality as a service on the cloud has forced us to consider that we need new political vocabularies thataddress the double bind of technical materiality and conceptual immateriality, as Seb Franklin argues.[11] But despite the social media industry–driven marketing campaigns for the cloud, we are as necessarily in need of technopolitical vocabularies of the geophysical and the underground, even in the context of clouds and data. The physicality of the internet became increasingly visible during 2013. In the wake of revelations of the NSA's spy program PRISM, the images of lonely data servers in the middle of nowhere gained new political currency; similarly, images of intelligence agencies such as depicted in Trevor Paglen's art became ways to imagine and investigate the global infrastructures of institutions whose own physical existence was confined to silent concrete buildings.[12]

But after Edward Snowden's whistleblowing what also surfaced was the case of Brazil: why was Brazil so much on the map of the surveillance operations of the American agency? The reason was quickly exposed: it was about the submarine cables. The paranoid surveillance mechanisms of the post–9/11 world of U.S. terror also highlight the extensive infrastructural arrangements of networks on the physical level. One of the main lines, Atlantis-2, connects South America to Europe and Africa,[13] allowing for a crucial interruption node to exist when *data arrives ashore*, to put it poetically. No wonder this has quickly spurred plans "to lay an undersea communications cable from Lisbon to Fortaleza"[14] just to bypass American interception.

We need to look at the underground realities as well as the submerged ones: not that different from the laying of the Atlantic cables in mid-nineteenth century. Back then the submerged media was escorted by an enthusiasm for interconnectedness. Now it is a secret enthusiasm for inter-ruptedness. The grounds, ungrounds, and undergrounds of media infrastructures condition what is visible and what is invisible. This is a question of power relations and contested territories in a way that makes the *geo-* in geopolitics stand out.[15] The earth is part of media both as a resource and as transmission. The earth conducts, also, literally, forming a special part of the media and sound artistic circuitry.[16] It is the contested political earth that extends to being part of military "infrastructure": the earth hides political stakes and can be formed as part of military strategy and maneuvers.

Notes

1. Antonio Stoppani, "First Period of the Anthropozoic Era," trans. Valeria Federeighi, ed. Etienne Turpin and Valeria Federeghi. In *Making the Geologic Now: Responses to the Material Conditions of Contemporary Life,* ed. Elizabeth Ellsworth and Jamie Kruse (New York: Punctum, 2013), 38.

2. John Durham Peters, "Space, Time, and Communication Theory," *Canadian Journal of Communication* 28, no. 4 (2003). http://www.cjc-online.ca/index.php/journal/article/view/1389/1467.

3. Sean Cubitt, "Electric Light and Electricity," Theory, Culture & Society 30, no. 7-8 (2013): 309–23.

4. Historical Statistics for Mineral and Material Commodities in the United States. U.S. Geological Survey Data Sets 140, <a href="http://minerals.usgs.gov/ds/2005/140/"http://minerals.usgs.gov/ds/2005/140/.

5. Elizabeth Grosz, *Chaos, Territory, Art: Deleuze and the Framing of the Earth* (New York: Columbia University Press, 2008), 10.

6. Benjamin Bratton, *The Stack* (forthcoming, MIT Press). Michael Nest, *Coltan* (Cambridge: Polity, 2011).

7. Robert Smithson, "A Sedimentation of the Mind: Earth Projects," in *Robert Smithson: The Collected Writings*, ed. Jack Flam (1968; Berkeley: University of California Press, 1996), 101. Of course, the resonance with Gregory Bateson's ideas from the 1960s and 1970s are explicit and thus a link to Guattari would be also interesting to map. See Bateson, *Steps to an Ecology of Mind* (St. Albans: Paladin, 1973).

8. Cf. Bruno Latour, *An Inquiry into Modes of Existence: An Anthropology of the Moderns,* trans. Catherine Porter (Cambridge, Mass.: Harvard University Press, 2013), 10.

9. Jennifer Gabrys, *Digital Rubbish: A Natural History of Electronics* (Ann Arbor: University of Michigan Press, 2011).

10. See also Jussi Parikka, "Insects and Canaries: Medianatures and the Aesthetics of the Invisible," *Angelaki* 18, no. 1 (2013): 107–19.

11. Seb Franklin, "Cloud Control, or the Network as a Medium," *Cultural Politics* 8, no. 3 (2012): 443–64.

12. On bunkers, besides Paul Virilio's work, see also John Beck, "Concrete Ambivalence: Inside the Bunker Complex," Cultural Politics 7, no. 1 (2011): 79–102.

13. "What the N.S.A. Wants in Brazil," *The New Yorker,* July 24 (2013). http://www.newyorker.com/online/blogs/newsdesk/2013/07/why-the-nsa-really-cares-about-brazil.html.

14. Robin Emmott, "Brazil, Europe Plan Undersea Cable to Skirt U.S. Spying," *Reuters,* February 24 (2014). http://www.reuters.com/.

15. On sea cables and infrastructural (in)visibility, see Nicole Starosielski, "'Warning: Do Not Dig': Negotiating the Visibility of Critical Infrastructures," Journal of Visual Culture 11, no. 1 (2012): 38–57 . See also Ryan Bishop, "Project 'Transparent Earth' and the Autoscope of Aerial Targeting: The Visual Geopolitics of the Underground," *Theory, Culture & Society* 28, no. 7–8 (2011): 270–86.

16. Douglas Kahn, *Earth Sound Earth Signal: Energies and Earth Magnitude in the Arts* (Berkeley: The University of California Press, 2013).

1

And the Earth Screamed, Alive

What if your guide to the world of media would not be the usual suspect—an entrepreneur or evangelista from Silicon Valley, or an aspirant from a management school hoping to catch up with the smooth crowd-sourced clouding of the network sphere? What if your guide were Professor Challenger, the Arthur Conan Doyle character from the 1928 short story "When the World Screamed"? The story appeared in the *Liberty* magazine and offered an odd insight into a mad scientist's world, with a hint of what we would nowadays call "speculative realism." Professor Challenger, whose dubious and slightly mad reputation preceded him, offered an insight to what later philosophers such as the French writing duo Gilles Deleuze and Félix Guattari happily picked up on: that the earth is alive, and its crust is tingling with life. But the idea of the living earth has a long cultural history too: from antiquity it persists as the idea of *terra mater*, and in the emerging mining cultures of the eighteenth and nineteenth centuries becomes embedded as part of Romantic philosophy; later in the twentieth century the emergence of Gaia theories brings a different connotation to the holistic life of the planet.

The narrative of strata and geology starts with a letter: an undated letter addressed to Mr. Peerless Jones, an expert in artesian drilling. The letter is a request for assistance. The nature of what is required is not specified, but the reputation of the mad scientist, the slightly volatile personality of Professor Challenger, promises that it would not be a normal operation. In an atmosphere of suspicion and curiosity, it soon becomes evident that Mr. Jones' drilling expertise is needed. In Sussex, U.K., at Hengist Down, Professor Challenger is engaged in a rather secret drilling operation; it is initially unclear what sort of a job the special drills are needed for. Even the sort of material to be penetrated is revealed only later to be different from what is usually expected from mining operations: not chalk or clay or the usual geological strata but more of a jelly-like substance.

The operation did not start with the undated letter. The Professor had been drilling deeper and deeper through the earth's crust until he had finally discovered a layer that pulsates like a living animal. That the earth is alive, and that this vitality can be proved with experimental means, was actually the true objective of Challenger's mission. Instead of drilling and mining for petroleum, coal, copper, iron ore, and other valuables for which men usually dig holes in the ground, Challenger's mission is driven by a desire to prove a new speculative position that concerns the living depths of the earth: beyond the strata of "sallow lower chalk, the coffee-coloured Hastings beds, the lighter Ashburnham beds, the dark carboniferous clays, and . . . gleaming in the electric light, band after band of jet-black, sparkling coal alternative with the rings of clay"[1] one finds unusual layers, which did not adhere to the classical geological theories of Hutton or Lyell. It seemed suddenly undeniable that even inorganic matter is alive: "The throbs were not direct, but gave the impression of a gentle ripple or rhythm, which ran across the surface,"[2] Mr. Jones describes the deep surface they found: "The surface was not entirely homogenous but beneath it, seen as through ground glass, there were dim whitish patches or vacuoles, which varied constantly in shape and size." The layers, the core and the strata, throbbed, pulsated, animated. One need not go to the same lengths as Professor Challenger does, in one of the most bizarre rape-like scenes in literature, when he penetrates that jellyesque layer just to make the earth scream. This scientific sadism echoes in the ears of the audience and much further. It is the sound of "a thousand of sirens in one, paralyzing all the great multitude with its fierce insistence, and floating away through the still summer air until it went echoing along the whole South Coast and even reach our French neighbors across the Channel."[3] All this was observed and witnessed by an audience called by the Professor—peers and interested international crowd, by invitation only.

The interest in "the bowels of the earth"[4] was not restricted to fiction writing and the vibrant language of Conan Doyle. Professor Challenger was predated by nineteenth-century fiction characters, like Heinrich in Novalis's *Heinrich von Ofterdingen* (1800/1802) asking "Is it possible that beneath our feet a world of its own is stirring in a great life?"[5] The poetic thrust toward the living pulsating earth opened it up: for coal, for minerals, for precious material. The earth had become a resource anyway. earth metals and minerals were tightly linked to the emergence of modern engineering, science, and technical media. Metals such as copper were a crucial material feature of technical media culture since the nineteenth century. A lot of the early copper mines, however, were exhausted by the start of the twentieth century, leading to new demands both in terms of international reach and in terms of depth. New drills were needed for deeper mining, which was necessary in order to provide the materials for an increasing international need for wires and network culture. The increasing demand and international reach of the industry resulted in the cartelization of the copper business from mining to smelting.[6] Indeed, beside such historical contexts of mining, where Challenger's madness starts to make sense, one is tempted to think of imaginary horrors of the underground, as depicted by writers from H. P. Lovecraft to Fritz Leiber. Leiber preempts a much more recent writer of the biopolitics of petroleum, Reza Negarestani, both highlighting the same theme: petroleum is a living subterranean life form.[7] One should not ignore the earth screams caused by hydraulic fracturing (fracking) that, beside the promise that it might change the geopolitical balance of energy production, points toward what is often neglected in the discourse of geopolitics: *geo*, the earth, the soil and depth of the crust that leads to the bowels of the earth. By pumping pressurized water and chemicals underground the procedure forces gas out from between rocks, forcing the earth to become an extended resource. Rocks fracture, benzene and formaldehyde creep in, and the earth is primed to expose itself. Fracking is, in the words of Brett Neilson, perfectly tuned to the capitalist hyperbole of expansion across limits: "Whether it derives from the natural commons of earth, fire, air, and water or the networked commons of human cooperation, fracking creates an excess that can be tapped."[8]

Inside the earth, one finds a metallic reality, which feeds into metal metaphysics and digital devices. Besides the speculative stance, one can revert back to empirical material too. In short, of direct relevance to our current media technological situation is the reminder that according to year 2008 statistics, media materiality is very metallic: "36 percent of all tin, 25 percent of cobalt, 15 percent of palladium, 15 percent silver, 9 percent of gold, 2 percent of copper, and 1 percent of aluminum"[9] goes annually to media technologies. We have shifted from being a society that until mid-twentieth century was based on a very restricted list of materials ("wood, brick, iron, copper, gold, silver, and a few plastics")[10] to one in which a computer chip is composed of "60 different elements."[11] Such lists of metals and materials of technology include rare earth minerals that are increasingly at the center of both global political controversies over tariffs and export restrictions from China. They are also related to the debates concerning the environmental damage caused by extensive open-pit mining massively reliant on chemical processes. Indeed, if the actual rock mined is likely to contain less than a percent of copper[12] it means that the pressure is on the chemical processes to tease out the *Cu* for further refined use in our technological devices.

The figures about metals for media seem astounding but testify to another materiality of technology that links with Conan Doyle but also with contemporary media arts discourse concerning the deep time of the earth. I will move on from Professor Challenger, however, to Siegfried Zielinski the German media studies professor, and his conceptualization of deep times of media art histories. In short, and what I shall elaborate in more detail soon, the figure of the deep time is for Zielinski a sort of a media archaeological gesture that while borrowing from paleontology actually turns out to be a riff for understanding the longer-term durations of art and science collaboration in Western and non-Western contexts. I want to argue, however, that there is a need for a more literal understanding and mobilization of deep times , in terms of depth as well as temporality, in media technological discourse and in relation to media art histories too. Professor Challenger is here to provide the necessary, even if slightly dubious, point about geological matter as living: this sort of a media history is of a speculative kind. It refers to a completely different time-scale than is usually engaged by our field. It borrows from the idea of dynamics of nonlinear history that Manuel Delanda so inspirationally mapped in terms of genes, language, and geology but which in this case can be approached even more provocatively as not just thousands, but millions and billions of years of nonlinear stratified media history.[13] Media history conflates with earth history; the geological material of metals and chemicals get deterritorialized from their strata and reterritorialized in machines that define our technical media culture.

The extension of life to inorganic processes follows from Deleuze and Guattari's philosophy. Life consists of dynamic patterns of variation and stratification. Stratification is a living double articulation that shows how geology is much more dynamic than dead matter. This is obviously an allusion to the reading one finds in Deleuze and Guattari's *A Thousand Plateaus*, in which the whole philosophical stakes of this enterprise are revealed. The intensities of the earth, the flows of its dynamic unstable matter, are locked into strata. This process of locking and capture is called stratification, and it organizes the molecular inorganic life into "molar aggregates."[14]

To ask a minor rhetorical question that detours via Deleuze and Guattari: what if we start our excavation of media technologies and digital culture not from Deleuze's often-quoted *Control Societies* text, but from Deleuze and Guattari's joint texts on geology and stratification?[15] This is the implicit task of this text, with a focus on the emerging critical discourse of resource depletion and minerals, and a harder materiality than hardware. Hardware perspectives are not necessarily hard enough, and if we want to extend our material notions of media thoroughly toward deeper materialities and deeper times, we need to be able to talk of the matter that contributes to the assemblages and durations of media as technology. This comes out most clearly in two ways. First, the research and design, fabrication and standardization of new materials that allow media processes and high technology processes to emerge. This relates to the history of chemistry as well as product development of synthetic materials as well as metals like aluminum that characterize modernity, alongside the work on material sciences that enabled so much of computer culture. Silicon and germanium are obvious examples of discoveries in chemistry that proved to be essential for computer culture. More recently, for instance, the minuscule 22 nanometer transistors that function without silicon are made of indium gallium arsenid; they demonstrate that a lot of science happens before the discursive wizardry of creative technology discourse. The MIT research project is allowing "evaporated indium, gallium, and arsenic atoms to react, forming a very thin crystal of InGaAs that will become the transistor's channel."[16] This short quote suffices to show that materiality of media starts long before media becomes media. Second, in a parallel fashion, we need to be able to discuss the media that is not media any longer. This is the other pole of media materiality: less high-tech, defined by obsolescence and depletion:[17] the mined rare earth minerals essential to computers and advanced technology industries from entertainment to the military, as well as, for instance, the residue products from the processes of fabrication, like the minuscule aluminum dust residue released from polishing iPad cases to be desirably shiny for the consumer market.[18]

Notes

1. Arthur Conan Doyle, "When the World Screamed" (1928). http://www.classic-literature.co.uk/scottish-authors/arthur-conan-doyle/when-the-world-screamed/ebook-page-10.asp.

2. Ibid., http://www.classic-literature.co.uk/scottish-authors/arthur-conan-doyle/when-the-world-screamed/ebook-page-11.asp.

3. Ibid., http://www.classic-literature.co.uk/scottish-authors/arthur-conan-doyle/when-the-world-screamed/ebook-page-14.asp. The allusion to rape is made even more obvious when considering the long-term mythological articulation of the earth with the female. The female interior of the earth is one of valuable riches. Steven Connor, *Dumbstruck: A Cultural History of Ventriloquism* (Oxford: Oxford University Press, 2000), 52.

4. Doyle, "When the World Screamed," http://www.classic-literature.co.uk/scottish-authors/arthur-conan-doyle/when-the-world-screamed/ebook-page-14.asp.

5. Novalis quoted in Theodore Ziolkowski, *German Romanticism and Its Institutions* (Princeton, N.J.: Princeton University Press, 1990), 31.

6. Richard Maxwell and Toby Miller, *Greening the Media* (Oxford: Oxford University Press, 2012), 55.

7. Fritz Leiber, "The Black Gondolier," in *The Black Gondolier and Other Stories*. E-Reads (2002). Reza Negarestani, *Cyclonopedia: Complicity with Anonymous Materials* (Melbourne: Re.Press, 2008). Eugene Thacker, "Black Infinity, or, Oil Discovers Humans," in *Leper Creativity* (New York: Punctum, 2012), 173–80.

8. Brett Neilson, "Fracking," in *Depletion Design*, ed. Carolin Wiedemann and Soenke Zehle (Amsterdam: Institute of Network Cultures and xm:lab, 2012), 85.

9. Maxwell and Miller, *Greening the Media*, 93.

10. T. E. Graedel, E. M. Harper, N. T. Nassar, and Barbara K. Reck, "On the Materials Basis of Modern Society," *PNAS*, October 2013, early edition: 1.

11. Ibid. See also Akshat Raksi, "The Metals in Your Smartphone May Be Irreplaceable," *Ars Technica*, December 5, 2013, http://arstechnica.com/science/2013/12/the-metals-in-your-smartphone-may-be-irreplaceable/.

12. Brett Milligan, "Space-Time Vertigo," in *Making the Geologic Now: Responses to the Material Conditions of Contemporary Life*, ed. Elizabeth Ellsworth and Jamie Kruse (New York: Punctum, 2013), 124.

13. Manuel Delanda, *A Thousand Years of Nonlinear History* (New York: Swerve/MIT Press, 2000). Delanda's argument for a geological approach to human history stems from an understanding of self-organization as the general drive behind how matter and energy are distributed. In this way, he is able to argue provocatively that "human societies are very much like lava flows" (55), referring to their nonlinear patterns of organization. In addition, he does well to shed light on the aspects of historical character in which there can be seen extensive continua between geological formations and what we tend to call human history—for instance, that of urbanity. Indeed, the processes of mineralization some 500 million years ago give rise to the endoskeleton and materiality of the bone affecting the processes crucial for the birth of humans (and a range of other specific types of bony organic life), as well as later affording a range of other processes. Indeed, Delanda talks of the exoskeleton of urban cities as being made possible by this same process, and tracks how metals, for instance, play their parts in the formation of urban centralization and clustering. We could in this vein argue that the processes of mineralization extend to the current computer age too, in terms of how the sedimented but deterritorializing layers of geological time are making possible a further exoskeleton—an argument that has its implicit resonances with the way in which, for instance, Bernard Stiegler has pitched the various externalizations of human memory, leaning on Edmund Husserl and Gilbert Simondon.

14. Gilles Deleuze and Félix Guattari, *A Thousand Plateaus*, trans. Brian Massumi (Minneapolis: University of Minnesota Press, 1987), 40. They are adamant in emphasizing that this is not a matter of substance and form (the hylomorphic model persistent in philosophy), the dualism usually haunting the linguistically modeled idea of meaning. Instead they want to introduce a geologically driven idea of the materiality of

signification, including asignifying elements. The double nature of the articulation is expressed as follows: "The first articulation chooses or deducts, from unstable particle-flows, metastable molecular or quasi-molecular units (*substances*)upon which it imposes a statistical order of connections and successions (*forms*). The second articulation establishes functional, compact, stable structures (*forms*), and constructs the molar compounds in which these structures are simultaneously actualized (*substances*).In a geological stratum, for example, the first articulation is the process of 'sedimentation,' which deposits units of cyclic sediment according to a statistical order: flysch, with its succession of sandstone and schist. The second articulation is the 'folding' that sets up a stable functional structure and effects the passage from sediment to sedimentary rock" (40–41). A good and necessary philosophical reading of the geological is Ben Woodard's *On an Ungrounded Earth: Towards a New Geophilosophy* (New York: Punctum, 2013). It offers a critique and expansion of the Deleuze-Guattarian perspective. Also important is Manuel Delanda's earlier text "The Geology of Morals: A Neomaterialist Interpretation," *Virtual Futures* 95 (1995). http://www.t0.or.at/delanda/geology.htm.

15. In short, in *A Thousand Plateaus* Deleuze and Guattari pitch the idea of geology of morals (a reference to Nietzsche) as illuminating an idea of stratification as a double articulation. Endnote 30 clarified this aspect. Such a process, however, is not restricted to geology, but allows Deleuze and Guattari to talk of geology of morals. In my further development, geology of media is, besides a philosophical figure and a nod toward *A Thousand Plateaus*, an emerging perspective of the careful selection and sedimentation of certain material elements necessary for the consolidation of functional media technologies. Such technologies express continua between nature and culture, or what I have called *medianatures*, which often signal themselves through ecological implications, or to be frank, problems—energy production, waste, and so forth. For Delanda, the Deleuze and Guattari geological model provides a new materialism of stratification that as an abstract machine runs across various materialities: "sedimentary rocks, species and social classes (and other institutionalized hierarchies) are all historical constructions, the product of definite structure-generating processes that take as their starting point a heterogeneous collection of raw materials (pebbles, genes, roles), homogenize them through a sorting operation, and then consolidate the resulting uniform groupings into

a more permanent state" (Delanda, "Geology of Morals," 62). On "medianatures," see Jussi Parikka, "Media Zoology and Waste Management: Animal Energies and Medianatures," *Necsus-European Journal of Media Studies* 4 (2013), http://www.necsus-ejms.org/.

16. Sebastian Anthony, "MIT Creates Tiny, 22nm Transistor Without Silicon," *Extremetech*, December 11, 2012. http://www.extremetech.com/extreme/143024-mit-creates-tiny-22nm-transistor-without-silicon.

17. See Wiedemann and Zehle, eds., *Depletion Design* (Amsterdam: Institute of Network Cultures and xm:lab, 2012).

18. Jussi Parikka, "Dust and Exhaustion: The Labor of Media Materialism," *Ctheory*, October 2, 2013, http://www.ctheory.net/articles.aspx?id=726.

2

Zielinski's notion of *Tiefenzeit*, deep time, is itself an attempt to use the idea of geological times to guide the way in which we think of the humanities-focused topics of media arts and digital culture. Deep time carries a lot of conceptual gravity, and is employed as a way to investigate the "Deep Time of Technical Means of Hearing and Seeing." Zielinski's approach kicks off as a critique of a teleological notion of media evolution that assumes a natural progress embedded in the narratives of the devices—a sort of a parasitical attachment, or insistence on the rationality of the machines and digital culture, that of course has had its fair share of critique during the past decades of media and cultural studies. We could call this "mythopoesis"[1] (to borrow a notion from a different context of the Ippolita-group), which as a critical perspective focuses on the narratives of (and in technology as the site of) political struggle. Zielinski's media-archaeological (and *anarchaeological*) approach, however, focuses on geological time.

For Zielinski, earth times and geological durations become a theoretical strategy of resistance against the linear progress myths that impose a limited context for understanding technological change. It relates in parallel to the early modern discussions concerning the religious temporal order vis-à-vis the growing "evidence of immense qualitative geological changes"[2] which articulated the rift between some thousands of years of biblical time and the millions of years of earth history.

This deep temporality combined the spatial and temporal. Indeed, in James Hutton's *Theory of the Earth* from 1778, depth means time: under the layers of granite you find further strata of slate signaling the existence of deep temporalities. Hutton is proposing a radical immensity of time although it comes without a promise of change; all is predetermined as part of a bigger cycle of erosion and growth.[3] Despite his use of terms such as "continual succession" for time of the earth and its geological cycles discovered in its strata (the reading of strata, "stratigraphy") time of immense durations does not change in the historical fashion. More specifically and in Hutton's words:

> The immense time necessarily required for this total destruction of the land, must not be opposed to that view of future events, which is indicated by the surest facts, and most approved principles. Time, which measures every thing in our idea, and is often deficient to our schemes, is to nature endless and as nothing; it cannot limit that by which alone it had existence; and, as the natural course of time, which to us seems infinite, cannot be bounded by any operation that may have an end, the progress of things upon this globe, that is, the course of nature, cannot be limited by time, which must proceed in a continual succession.[4]

Hutton continues to discuss and consider "the globe of this earth as a machine, constructed upon chemical as well as mechanical principles" as well as an organized body that proceeds through times of decay and repair. Hutton proposes a view and a theory of the earth as one of cycles and variations:

> His theory posited that the earth was constantly restoring itself. He based this concept on a fundamental cycle: erosion of the present land, followed by the deposition of eroded grains (or dead ocean organisms) on the sea floor, followed by the consolidation of those loose particles into sedimentary rock, followed by the raising of those rocks to form new land, followed by erosion of the new land, followed by a complete repeat of the cycle, over and over again. Hutton was also the first to recognize the profound importance of subterranean heat, the phenomenon that causes volcanoes, and he argued that it was the key to the uplifting of formerly submerged land.[5]

As becomes clear later in Lyell's classic account of geology, this articulates a division in terms of the geological vs. the historical.[6] For Lyell, Hutton's assumption of the cyclical deep times becomes a research tool to understand the radical temporality of the earth. Lyell was definitely interested in change in ways that did not pertain to Hutton,[7] but this historicity was still of a different order from that of the emerging history disciplines focused on the hermeneutic worlds of the human. The different sets of knowledge formations pertaining to the natural and to the moral are also the context for two different modes of temporal order. The time of human concerns differs from geological time, which is argued to be a radical dynamic force that affects life across the boundaries of the organic and the inorganic. And yet it was a necessity to keep these separated, despite the fact that modern institutions were increasingly interested durations that surpassed the human: geological and biological (in sciences of the evolution). In creative cultural theory, we have recently seen inspiring accounts that connect feminist ontology with Charles

Darwin's temporal ontology of open-ended becoming through evolution.[8] We already mentioned the work of Grosz and should include how such influential thinkers such as Rosi Braidotti have built on the anthropocene discussions to connect them to a wider geocentric perspective, which orders us to rethink fundamental notions of subjectivity, community, and political attachment. For Braidotti, the notion is to be connected to ongoing struggles involving postcolonial and feminist agendas as well as to avoid technophobia and nostalgic homeostatic fantasies of the earth. One could claim that some of the radicalization of the temporal ontology already started with Hutton and Lyell.[9] Time is imagined beyond biblical restrictions, but tied to a view of a grand cycle that with Lyell led to the master trope of uniformitarianism.[10]

But neither Hutton's nor Lyell's theory is a stable ground for a more radical and nonlinear account of time for contemporary cultural and media theory. Indeed, it displaced biblical time by positing the earth as a transcendent entity outside historical change. Hutton's worldview was deistic and for him the world was a perfectly designed machine.[11] Hutton's geological world is also without change and difference, and works in cyclical temporeality.[12] It is no wonder then, as Simon Schaffer points out, that Hutton's account inspired Adam Smith's ideas concerning the invisible hand of capitalism in the emerging industrial system.[13] Both seemed to believe in universal laws governing the empirical world. The embedded cyclicality creates a fruitful opening to erosions and renewals. For Zielinski geological metaphors offer a way to investigate technological culture, but for Hutton, the planet *is* a machine. It is, however, one modeled on the steam engines of his age, primarily the Newcomen engine; its principles of expansion of steam inspired Hutton with the idea of elevation of the crust.[14] This machine also assumes organic unity and cyclical renewal, and feeds off the heat at its core.[15]

Such ideas inspired various visualizations of the deep time of the earth. The deeper strata and their remaining layers, including fossils, signal time as well: the planet is structured according to a depth of the temporal past. These layers structure animal and human life, but also the industrial system of production and the technological culture of human civilization. But this is exactly where Zielinski also departs. Paradoxically, Hutton's inspiration (and he was only one of the geotheorists working on this topic in his time) goes toward both the universalizing and standardizing logic of the industrial factory system and Zielinski's exactly opposite account of variantology, which finds an alternative tune with Stephen Jay Gould. Indeed, through Gould, Zielinski is able to carve out a more detailed account of what the geological idea affords to media art history and media analysis as variantology.

In order to achieve this, Zielinski has to turn from Hutton to more contemporary readings of geology and paleontology. Zielinski picks up on Gould's paleontological explanations and ideas, which emphasize the notion of variation. It is in Gould's *Time's Arrow, Time's Cycle* that Zielinski finds an account suitable to a critique of progress in media culture. As a reader of Gould, Zielinski notes that the quantifying notion of deep times is itself renewed with a qualitative characteristic that produces a critique of myths of progress, which present a linear imagination of the world. Both discover the need to evacuate divinity from the cosmological picture, whether one of the earth or the media. Instead one has to develop images, metaphors, and iconography that do not reproduce illusions of linear progress "from lower to higher, from simple to complex."[16] A resurgent emphasis on diversity takes the place of the too neatly stacked historical layers.

Without going too much into the geologic debates, we need to understand how Gould's note itself is based on his arguments against uniformitarianism. Gould's argument for "punctuated equilibrium" is targeted against the false assumption of a continuous, uniform evolution which persisted in the various geological and evolutionary accounts for a long time. It includes Lyell's views as much as Darwin's beliefs.[17] The series of arguments and academic discussions Gould started together with his co-writer Niles Eldredge stems from the early 1970s, and also included both a new way of approaching the fossil record and a different understanding of temporal ontology as part of geology.[18] In short, to counteract the view that one can read a slow evolutionary change from the geological records, which have gaps and missing parts, one must approach this "archive" in a different way. The imaginary for this begins in the nineteenth century: processes of transmission and recording are already present in the earth itself, a vast library waiting to be deciphered.[19] The idea of punctuated equilibrium, however, suggested that instead of a constant uniform speed for change and evolution, the fossil record might show changes occurring at different speeds: from slow evolutions to sudden jolts or jumps. The processes of speciation and variation are not one-speed only but more of a multitemporal mix, with singular points that punctuate the evolution in specific ways.

Already this short elaboration reveals the wider scientific stakes in Gould and Eldredge's account: it offered a different theoretical understanding of time in geology. For Zielinski, this enabled a way to understand media archaeology as also having deep times. In these depths could be found the roots of the ways in which we modify, manipulate, create, and recreate means of hearing and seeing. Zielinski introduces inspirational deep times of apparata, ideas and solutions for mediatic desires that take inventors as the gravity point. He himself admits this approach is perhaps romantic, and focused paradoxically on human heroes. It includes figures such as Empedocles (of Four Elements fame), Athananius Kircher, and, for instance, the operatic dreams of Joseph Chudy and his early audiovisual telegraph system from the late eighteenth century (he composed a one-act opera on the topic: *The Telegraph or the Tele-Typewriter*). They also include the opium-fueled media desires of the slightly masochistically inclined Jan Evangelista Purkyne, a Czech from the early nineteenth century in the habit of using his own body for various drug- and electricity-based experiments to see how the body itself is a creative medium. What we encounter are variations that define alternative deep-time strata of our media culture outside the mainstream. It offers the anarchaeology of surprises and differences, of the uneven in media's cultural past, revealing a different aspect of a possible future. Zielinski's project is parallel to imaginations of "archaeologies of the future"[20] that push us to actively invent other futures.

Zielinski's methodology offers a curious paradox in terms of the general paleontological framing. The deep-time metaphor acts as a passage to map different times and spaces of media art history. Even the term connotes the darker underground of hidden fluxes that surface only irregularly to give a taste of the underbelly of a deep media history.[21] They offer variation in the sense Zielinski is after in media variantology: media do not progress from simple to complex; there are no blueprints for prediction; and we need to steer clear of the "psychopathia medialis" of standardization and to find points of variation to promote diversity. This is not meant to signal conservation as a desired strategy but active diversification as a strategy of a living cultural heritage of technological pasts in the present-futures.[22]

In any case, while Zielinski's metaphorics are fascinating, I would suggest care in picking up on their more concrete geological implications. With a theoretical hard hat on, I wonder if there is actually more to be found in this use of the notion of deep time both as temporality and as geological materiality. Perhaps this renewed use offers a variation that reattaches the concepts to discussions concerning media materialism as well as the political geology of contemporary media culture as reliant on the metals and minerals of the earth. Hence, the earth time gradually systematized by Hutton and other geotheorists of his period sustains the media time we are interested in. In other words, the heat-engine cosmology of earth times that Hutton provides as a starting point for a media-art historical theory of later times is one that also implicitly contains other aspects we need to reemphasise in the context of the anthrobscene: the machine of the earth is one that lives off its energy sources, in a similar way that our media devices and the political economy of digital culture are dependent on energy (cloud computing is still to a large extent powered by carbon emission–heavy energy production)[23] and materials (metals, minerals, and a long list of refined and synthetic components). The earth is a machine of variation, and media can live off variation—but both earth and media are machines that need energy and are tied together in their dynamic feedback loop. Electronic waste is an example of how media feeds back to earth history and future fossil times.

The main question that Zielinski's argument raises is this: besides the media variantological account concerning the design of apparatuses, users, desires, expressions, and different ways of processing the social order and means of seeing and hearing . . . there is this other deep time too. This sort of alternative is more literal in the sense of returning to the geological stratifications and to a Professor Challenger–type of excavation, deeper into the living ground. Geological interest since the eighteenth and nineteenth centuries produced the concept that was later coined "deep time," but we need to be able to understand that the new mapping of geology and the earth's resources was the political economic function of this emerging epistemology. This is where archaeological and geological interests reveal the other sides of deep time: sides that expose the earth as party to new connections. Indeed, the knowledge of the earth through geological specimens (demonstrated, for instance, in Diderot and D'Alembert's "Mineral Lodes or Veins and Their Bearings" in volume 6 of *l'Éncylopedie* in 1768) and its newly understood history meant a new relation between esthetics and the sciences. This link is also beneficial for inventing new ways of extracting value: "As a result of eighteenth-century archeological and antiquarian activities, the earth acquired a new perceptual depth, facilitating the conceptualization of the natural as immanent history, and of the earth's materials as resources that could be extracted just like archeological artifacts."[24]

The media theoretical deep time divides into two related directions:

1. Geology refers to the affordances that enable digital media to exist as a materially complex realm of production and process mediated by political economics: a metallic materiality that links the earth to the media-technological.

2. Temporalities such as deep time are understood in this alternative account as concretely linked to the nonhuman earth times of decay and renewal but also to the current anthropocene of the obscenities of the ecocrisis. Or to put it in one word: the *anthrobscene.*

Deep temporalities[25] expand to media theoretical trajectories: such ideas and practices force media theory outside the usual scope of media studies in order to look at the wider milieu in which media materially and politically become media in the first place. This relates to Peters's speculative question about cosmology, science, and media, which turns into a short historical mapping of how astronomy and geology are susceptible to being understood as media disciplines of a sort.[26] Continuing Peters's idea we can further elaborate geophysics' degree zero of media technological culture. It allows media to take place, and has to carry their environmental load. Hence this "geology of media" perspective expands to the earth and its resources. It summons a media ecology of the inorganic, and it picks up from Matthew Fuller's notes on "media ecology as a cascade of parasites"[27] as well as an "affordance" itself allowed by a range of processes and techniques that involve the continuum of the biological-technological-geological.

Notes

1. Ippolita and Tiziana Mancinelli, "The Facebook Aquarium: Freedom in a Profile," in *Unlike Us Reader: Social Media Monopolies and Their Alternatives*, ed. Geert Lovink and Miriam Rasch (Amsterdam: Institute of Network Cultures, 2013), 164.

2. Zielinski, *Deep Time of the Media: Toward an Archaeology of Hearing and Seeing by Technical Means*, trans. Gloria Custance (Cambridge, Mass.: The MIT Press, 2006), 3.

3. Stephen Jay Gould, *Time's Arrow, Time's Cycle: Myth and Metaphor in the Discovery of Geological Time* (Cambridge, Mass.: Harvard University Press, 1987), 86–91.

4. James Hutton, *Theory of the Earth*, e-version on Project Gutenberg, 1792/ 2004, online at http://www.gutenberg.org/.

5. Jack Repchek, *The Man Who Invented Time: James Hutton and the Discovery of Earth's Antiquity* (New York: Basic Books, 2009), 8.

6. Charles Lyell, *Principles of Geology* (London: John Murray, 1830), 1–4. ?Online facsimile at http://www.esp.org/books/lyell/principles/ facsimile/.

7. Stephen Jay Gould, *Time's Arrow, Time's Cycle*, 167; 150–55.

8. Elizabeth Grosz, *Becoming Undone: Darwinian Reflections on Life, Politics, and Art* (Durham, N.C.: Duke University Press, 2011).

9. See Repchek, *The Man Who Invented Time*. Repchek presents Hutton as an important discoverer, but some of this discourse focusing on the originality of Hutton neglects earlier geological research that does not always pertain to a Christian worldview of limited biblical proportions. Furthermore, the invention of modern time in historiography follows slightly differing paths, opening up the idea of an open, radically different future. See Reinhart Koselleck, *Futures Past: On the Semantics of Historical Time*, trans. Keith Tribe (New York: Columbia University Press, 2004), 240–43.

10. Gould, *Time's Arrow, Time's Cycle*.

11. Martin J. S. Rudwick, *Bursting the Limits of Time: The Reconstruction of Geohistory in the Age of Revolution* (Chicago: University of Chicago Press, 2005), 160. Hutton's world does not allow for the accidental but remains in the natural theological view of an orderly universe.

12. Stephen Jay Gould, *Time's Arrow, Time's Cycle*, 87.

13. Simon Schaffer, "Babbage's Intelligence," online at http://www.imaginaryfutures.net/2007/04/16/babbages-intelligence-by-simon-schaffer/.

14. Rudwick, *Bursting the Limits*, 161.

15. Ibid., 159–62.

16. Zielinski, *Deep Time of the Media*, 5.

17. Stephen Jay Gould, *Punctuated Equilibrium* (Cambridge, Mass.: Harvard University Press, 2007), 10.

18. Niles Eldredge and Stephen Jay Gould, "Punctuated Equilibria: An

Alternative to Phyletic Gradualism," in *Models in Paleobiology*, ed. T. J. M. Schopf. (San Francisco: Freeman Cooper, 1972), 82–115.

19. Peters, "Space, Time, and Communication Media."

20. Fredric Jameson, *Archaeologies of the Future* (London: Verso, 2005).

21. See Alexander R. Galloway, Eugene Thacker, and McKenzie Wark, *Excommunication: Three Inquiries in Media and Mediation* (Chicago: Chicago University Press, 2013), 139.

22. Zielinski has continued these discussions in the Variantology book series as well as in the recently translated [... After the Media], trans. Gloria Custance (Minneapolis: Univocal, 2013).

23. The figures as to exactly how much network computing and data centers consume varies a lot, as well as the dependence on carbon emission–heavy energy. Peter W. Huber, "Dig More Coal, the PCs Are Coming," *Forbes*, May 31, 1999. Duncan Clark and Mike Berners-Lee, "What's the Carbon Footprint of . . . The Internet?" *The Guardian*, August 12, 2010. http://www.theguardian.com/. Seán O'Halloran, "The Internet Power Drain," *Business Spectator*, September 6, 2012. http://www.businessspectator.com.au/article/2012/9/6/technology/internet-power-drain.

24. Amy Catania Kulper, "Architecture's Lapidarium," in *Architecture in the Anthropocene. Encounters among Design, Deep Time, Science, and Philosophy*, ed. Etienne Turpin (Ann Arbor, Mich.: Open Humanities Press, 2013), 100.

25. Recent media and cultural theory has in most interesting ways picked up the notion of temporality again. In media archaeology it has emerged with a nonnarrative and nonhuman understanding of temporalities—for instance, microtemporality (Wolfgang Ernst). For Ernst, microtemporalities define the ontological basis of how media as reality production works in speeds with limited access to the human senses. Hence Ernst also has written about "temporealities." See Wolfgang Ernst, *Chronopoetik. Zeitweisen und Zeitgaben technischer Medien* (Berlin: Kadmos, 2013). See also Wolfgang Ernst, "From Media History to Zeitkritik," trans. Guido Schenkel. *Theory, Culture & Society* 30, no. 6 (2013): 132–46. In a slightly similar fashion Mark Hansen's recent work has flagged the need to embed media theoretical vocabulary in a different regime of sensation than conscious perception. In Hansen's Whitehead-inspired perspective, the limitations of phenomenology are worked through so as

to address the current ubiquitous digital media culture and the speeds at which it folds as part of the human, without being accessible through human senses. See Mark B. N. Hansen, *Feed Forward: On the Future of the Twenty-first Century Media* (Chicago: University of Chicago Press, forthcoming 2014). At the other scale, the duration of climatic and geological timescales has to be addressed. Besides this book on geology, see Claire Colebrook on extinction and the weird temporalities of nature and knowledge of nature. Colebrook, "Framing the End of Species," in *Extinction: Living Books about Life* (London: Open Humanities Press, 2011), http://www.livingbooksaboutlife.org/books/Extinction/Introduction.

26. Peters, "Space, Time, and Communication Media."

27. Matthew Fuller, *Media Ecologies: Materialist Energies in Art and Technoculture* (Cambridge, Mass.: The MIT Press, 2005), 174.

3

A Media History of Matter: From Scrap Metal to Zombie Media

Throughout this essay I am interested in alternative accounts of how to talk about the materiality of media technology. One aspect, with a concrete ecological edge, is the acknowledgment of the growing waste problem resulting from discarded media technologies. And another aspect relates to energy and power as already mentioned above.[1] Indeed, what I want to map as the alternative deep time relates to geology in the fundamental sense of the anthropocene. Crutzen's original pitch offered it as a transversal map across various domains: from nitrogen fertilizers in the soil to nitric oxide in the air; carbon dioxide and the condition of the oceans; photochemical smog to global warming. (Is photochemical smog the true new visual media form of post–World War II technological polluted culture?) Already Crutzen had initiated the expansive way of understanding "anthropocene" to be about more than geology. In Crutzen's initiating definitions it turned into a concept investigating the radical transformations in the living conditions of the planet.

The anthropocene can be said to be—in the way the German media philosopher Erich Hörl suggests referring to Deleuze—a concept that maps the scope of a transdisciplinary problem. So what is the problem? Hörl's suggestion is important.[2] He elaborates the anthropocene as a concept that responds to specific questions posed by the technological situation. It is about the environmental aspects but completely tied to the technological: this concept as well as its object are enframed by technological conditions into which we should be able to develop a further elaborated insight with the tools and conceptual arsenal of the humanities. Indeed, this is where a geology of media can offer necessary support as a conceptual bridge between chemical and metallic materials and the political economy and cultural impact of media technologies as part of the discourses of the ongoing global digital economy.

The concept of anthropocene becomes radically environmental. It does not mean purely a reference to "nature" but an environmentality understood and defined by the "technological condition."[3] The environmental expands from a focus on the natural ecology to an entanglement with technological questions, notions of subjectivity and agency (as a critique of the human-centered worldview) and a critique of such accounts of rationality that are unable to talk about nonhumans as constitutive of social relations. The anthropocene is a way to demonstrate that geology does not refer exclusively to the ground under our feet. It is constitutive of social and technological relations as well as environmental and ecological realities. Geology is deterritorialized in the concrete ways in which metal and minerals become mobile, and enable technological mobility: Benjamin Bratton's words could not be any more apt when he writes of how we carry small pieces of Africa in our pockets, referring to the role of, say, coltan in digital media technologies.[4] Also apt is when visual artist Paglen sees the geo-orbital layers of satellite debris as outer reaches of earth's geology and the anthropocene (The Last Pictures project).

iPhones are, in the words of *mammolith*, an architectural research and design platform, "geological extracts" drawing across the globe earth resources and supported by a multiplicity of infrastructures. The bits of earth you carry around are not restricted to small samples of Africa but include material from the Red Dog pit mine in Alaska (zinc ores) which are then refined into indium in Trail, Canada. But that's only small part of it, and such sites, where material gradually becomes media, are "scattered across the globe in the aforementioned countries, as well as South Korea, Belgium, Russia, and Peru."[5] An analysis of dead media should also take into account this aspect of the earth, and its relation to global logistics and production.

More concretely, let's focus for a while on China—but China understood as part of the global chains of production and abandonment of media technologies. This geopolitical China is not solely about the international politics of trade and labor (which are not to be neglected either). In a sense, we can focus on the material production of what then ends up as the massive set of consumer gadgets, and the future fossil record for a robot media archaeologist, but also as discarded waste: both electronic waste and scrap metals, necessary for booming urban building projects and industrial growth. So much of this is driven by the entrepreneurial attitude of optimism: of seeing the world in terms of material and immaterial malleability, which in the case of media technologies has been recently realized also to include hardware in new ways. Indeed, in the midst of the wider enthusiasm for a global digital economy of software, some business correspondents such as Jay Goldberg have realized that hardware is dirt cheap and even "dead."[6] His claim is less related to the Bruce Sterling–initiated proposal for a Handbook of Deadmedia, "A naturalist's field guide for the communications palaeontologist,"[7] than it is an acknowledgment of a business opportunity.

Goldberg's dead media business sense is focusing on the world of super-cheap tablet computers he first encounters in China and then in the U.S. for $40. In this particular story, it triggers a specific realization regarding business models and hardware: the latter becomes discardable, opening a whole new world of opportunities.

> When I show this tablet to people in the industry, they have universally shared my shock. And then they always ask "Who made it?" My stock answer is "Who cares?" But the truth of it is that I do not know. There was no brand on the box or on the device. I have combed some of the internal documentation and cannot find an answer. This is how far the Shenzhen electronics complex has evolved. The hardware maker literally does not matter. Contract manufacturers can download a reference design from the chip maker and build to suit customer orders. If I had 20,000 friends and an easy way to import these into the US, I would put my own name on it and hand them out as a business cards or Chanukah gifts.[8]

The reduced price of the tablets means widespread availability even for specified niche uses: from waitresses to mechanics, elderly people to kids, tablets could become the necessary accessory in visions that blow away when one realizes the business prospects. The Goldberg's visceral reaction is followed by rational calculations of what it might mean in the context of digital economy business models:

> Once my heart started beating again, the first thing I thought was,

"I thought the screen alone would cost more than $45." My next thought was, "This is really bad news for anyone who makes computing hardware. . . .

No one can make money selling hardware anymore. The only way to make money with hardware is to sell something else and get consumers to pay for the whole device and experience.[9]

Even hardware gets drawn into the discourse of experience economy with its connotations of immateriality. Hardware softens, becomes immaterialized, and its materiality seems to change before our eyes. What Goldberg misses is that hardware does *not* die, not even in the Sterling sense of unused dead media that becomes a sedimented layer of fossils left for quirky media archaeologists to excavate. Instead, it is abandoned, forgotten, stashed away, and yet retains a toxic materiality that surpasses the usual time scale we are used to in media studies. Such abandoned media devices are less about the time of use, or practices of users, but the time and practices of disuse. It would be interesting to write a history of cultural techniques of technological disuse. The chemical duration of metal materiality is also an important concept here. Think of this idea as the media technological equivalent of the half-life of nuclear material, calculated in hundreds and thousands of years of hazard; in media technological contexts, it refers to the dangerous materials inside screen and computing devices that are a risk to scrap workers as well as to nature, for instance, to the soil.

Next, look at the case from a different perspective. Adam Minter's journalistic report *Junkyard Planet* offers a different story of hard metals and work, and looks at the issue from the geology of scrap metals.[10] China is one of the key destinations, not only for electronic waste but scrap metals in general; this offers a different insight into the circulation of what we could call the geology of technologies. China's demand for materials is huge. Part of its continuing major push to build projects from buildings to subways to airports was the production or reprocessing of more metals: scrap copper, aluminium, steel, and more.:

> On the other side of the mall, in all directions, are dozens of new high-rises—all under construction—that weren't visible from the subway and my walk. Those new towers reach 20 and 30 stories, and they're covered in windows that require aluminum frames, filled with bathrooms accessorized with brass and zinc fixtures, stocked with stainless steel appliances, and—for the tech-savvy households—outfitted with iPhones and iPads assembled with aluminum backs. No surprise, China leads the world in the consumption of steel, copper, aluminum, lead, stainless steel, gold, silver, palladium, zinc, platinum, rare earth compounds, and pretty much anything else labeled "metal." But China is desperately short of metal resources of its own. For example, in 2012 China produced 5.6 million tons of copper, of which 2.75 million tons was made from scrap. Of that scrap copper, 70 percent was imported, with most coming from the United States. In other words, just under half of China's copper supply is imported as scrap metal. That's not a trivial matter: Copper, more than any other metal, is essential to modern life. It is the means by which we transmit power and information.

The wider picture of technological culture is not restricted to worried comments about the rare earth minerals essential to iPhones. The bigger picture becomes clear when we see the geology of technical media revealed by the phase it is in when it is discarded. The material history of media—for instance, telecommunications—extends to the copper extracted from wires, the outer covers stripped off to reveal this mini-mine of valuable media materials. The history of mining of copper with its environmentally dangerous effects is extended to the re-mining from wires for many novel repurposings. One could say, following Minter's narrative, that such a technological history of materials and material history of media as matter does not really follow a life-of-use to death-of-disuse logic. In places such as Foshan's Nanhai District, technologies and media materials never die: it is the place where scrap metal gets processed.[11]

In *Zombie Media* with Garnet Hertz we address the wider context and impact of the "dead media" devices refusing to disappear from planetary existence.[12] Building on Sterling's work, we argue that there is a need to account for the undead nature of obsolete media technologies and devices in at least two ways: to be able to remember that media never dies, but remains as toxic waste residue, and also that we should be able to repurpose and reuse solutions in new ways, as circuit bending and hardware hacking practices imply. The zombie media angle builds on two contexts not specific to digital media but present in such accounts as Goldberg's and the wider micropolitical stance that ties consumer desires with design practices. Planned obsolescence is one such feature we address, as do other art/hacking projects combining hardware hacking and circuit bending, such as Benjamin Gaulon's Recyclism. Such approaches take into account the current issue of abandoned hardware, which even in functional devices totals hundreds of millions of screens, mobiles, and electronic and computing technologies that still are not properly dealt with after their use. U.S. Environmental Protection Agency (EPA) statistics from 2013 describe 2.37 tons of electronics ready for their afterlife management, which represented "an increase of more than 120 percent compared to 1999."[13] The primary category is related to screen technologies, but we can safely assume that the rise of mobile technologies soon contributed a rather large share of this dead media pile, of which only 25 percent was collected for any sort of actual management and recycling in 2009. The amount of operational electronics discarded annually is one category of a geologically significant pile that entangles first, second, and third nature:[14] the communicational vectors of advanced digital technologies come with a rather direct link and impact to first natures, reminding that the contemporary reliance on swift communicational transactions is reliant on this aspect of hardware too. Those communicational events are sustained by the broader aspect of geology of media: technologies abandoned and consisting of hazardous material: lead, cadmium, mercury, barium, and more.

National, supranational and NGO bodies are increasingly forced to think the future of media and information technologies as something "below the turf." This means both a focus on the policies and practices of e-waste as one of the crucial areas of concern, and planning towards raw material extraction and logistics to ensure supply. As the above short mention of scrap metal in China illustrated, the usual practices of mining are not considered the only route for future geology of media. In any case, the future geo(physical)politics of media circulate around China, Russia, Brazil, Congo, and South Africa as key producers of raw materials. This politics connects to a realization that the materiality of information technology starts from the soil and the underground. Miles of crust opened up by sophisticated drills. This depth marks the passage from the mediasphere to the lithosphere. An increasing amount of critical materials are found only by going down deeper into the crust or otherwise difficult-to-reach areas. Offshore oil drilling is an example of this: the Tupi deposits of oil off the shore of Brazil, beneath "1.5 miles of water and another 2.5 miles of compressed salt, sand and rock;"[15] new methods of penetrating rocks by fracturing them or by using steam-assisted cavity drainage; deep sea mining by countries such as China; the list could be continued. Corporations such as Chevron boast of depth records for their mining—tens of thousands of feet under the ocean bottom[16] in search of oil as well as minerals. Suddenly an image comes to mind, one familiar from an earlier part of this essay: Professor Challenger's quest to dig deeper inside the crust that is alive.

Depth becomes not only an index of time but also a resource, in the fundamental sense of Martin Heidegger's standing reserve: technology reveals nature in ways that can turn it into a resource as well. For Heidegger, the writer of trees, rivers, and forest paths, the Rhine turns from *Hölderlin*'s poetic object into a technological construct effected in the assemblage of the new hydroelectric plant. The question of energy becomes a way of defining the river, and in Heideggerian terms, transforming it:

> The revealing that rules throughout modern technology has the character of a setting-upon, in the sense of a challenging-forth. That challenging happens in that the energy concealed in nature is unlocked, what is unlocked is transformed, what is transformed is stored up, what is stored up is, in turn, distributed, and what is distributed is switched about ever anew. Unlocking, transforming, storing, distributing, and switching about are ways of revealing.[17]

This notion of transformation becomes a central way to understand the technological assemblages in which metals and minerals are mobilized as part of technological and media contexts. Technology constructs new pragmatic and epistemological realms where geology turns into a media resource. And similarly geology itself transforms into a contested technologically conditioned object of research and a concept that we are able to use to understand the widespread mobilization of nature. It also transforms questions of deep times from the merely temporal past to futures of extinction, pollution, and resource depletion, triggering a huge chain of events and interlinked questions: the future landscape of media technological fossils.

This transformation of geology of media, and media of geology/metals works in a couple of directions. Theorists, policy makers and even politicians are increasingly aware of the necessity of cobalt, gallium, indium, tantalum and other metals and minerals for media technological ends, from end user devices like mobiles and game consoles to more generally capacitors, displays, batteries and so forth. In short, the geophysics of media consists of examples such as:

Cobalt: Lithium-ion batteries, synthetic fuels
Gallium: Thin layer photovoltaics, IC, WLED
Indium: Displays, thin layer photovoltaics
Tantalum: Micro capacitors, medical technology
Antimony: ATO, micro capacitors
Platinum: Fuel cells, catalysts
Palladium: Catalysts, seawater desalination
Niobium: Microcapacitors, ferroalloys
Neodymium: Permanent magnets, laser technology
Germanium: Fiber optic cable, IR optical technologies[18]

Moments of deep time are exposed in such instances as Clemens Winkler's 1885/1886 discovery of Germanium (named of course after his home country) when he was able to distinguish it from antimony.[19] Winkler's discovery in Freiberg is certainly a part of the history of chemistry and the elements, but it also initiates insights into computer culture, where the semiconducting capacities of this specific alloy competed with what we now consider a key part of our computer culture: silicon. But such deep times are also telling a story of the underground . . .

which is not to be confused with a discourse of underground art and activism, as we so often revert back to in media art-historical discourse. This new definition of media deep time is more in tune with mining and transportation, of raw material logistics and processing, and refining of metals and minerals. The underground haunts the military imaginary and reality through the geography of bunkers, guerrilla trenches, and passages (such as those used by the Viet Cong) as well as the nuclear silos that are burrowed into the landscapes of the U.S.;[20] and it haunts the technological reality of modernity. The underground has, since the nineteenth century at least, been the site of imagined technological futures, as Rosalind Williams shows,[21] but it is also the actual site of technological development.[22]

To reiterate the argument: The long historical durations of deep time as introduced to media art discussions by Zielinski take place in antique times, with medieval alchemists and in nineteenth-century science-art collaborations as exemplary events of deep time media artistic techniques and ideas. But what if we need to account for an alternative deep time, which extends deeper toward a geophysics of media culture? This is a possibility not to be missed: an alternative media history of matter. Such a geophysics extends the historical interest in alchemists to contemporary mining practices, minerals, and the subsequent materialities. Would this sort of approach be something that is comfortable to tackle with materiality below the ground level (such theory is definitely "*low theory*," to refer to McKenzie Wark's notion),[23] stretched between political economy of resources and art practices (as we will see in the next chapter more clearly).

The geology of media that nods toward Zielinski but wants to extend deep times toward chemical and metal durations includes a wide range of examples of refined minerals, metals, and chemicals that are essential for media technologies to deliver audiovisual content in miniaturized form. *Understanding Media* is complemented with the duration of materials as significant for media temporality.[24] In other words, we don't just *understand* media but it has other material effects and affects as well.

The interactions of chemicals, material sciences, and technical media were never really forgotten in such accounts as Friedrich Kittler's. His media-historical insights often took account of the grounding role that material sciences and discoveries have in enabling both media technologies and military operations. Hence his attention to such details as a blockade of Chilean nitrate to Germany[25] by the telegraphically effective British naval troops in World War I lays out as a story the geopolitical importance of sodium nitrate mining in Chile, and the necessary substitute of synthetic ammoniac through the chemical innovation of Haber and Bosh, as it was needed for German munitions production. Technologies are matters of war and logistics; these categories bring the particular Kittler-perspective to bear on a media history of matter:

> For over a century, wars and technologies have dreamed of being ahead of their day. In reality, however, they are forced to engage in recursions that burrow into ever deeper pasts. Lack of nitrate scuttled Alfred von Schlieffen's ingenious plan of attack. Just as up-to-date computer design is steadily closing in on the big bang, the logistics of war (irrespective of wishful ecological thinking) consume ever-older resources. The Second World War began with the switch from coal and railroads to tank oil and airplane fuel, the Pax Americana with the exploration of uranium (in Germany, the task was assigned to Hans-Martin Schleyer).[26]

The history of fertilizers meets in this chemical conjunction the history of war and technological culture. The thousands of years of cultural techniques of manipulating the soil for purposes of agriculture reaches one sort of a singular point by World War I, but also shows how histories of the anthropocene entangle with histories of war and technology, where the latter have been discussed in media theory and history. But in this context, as already hinted at some points in earlier chapters, the chemical constitution of technological culture is not to be neglected. Industrialization becomes a point of synchronization of various lineages of cultural techniques. The agricultural metaphor of "culturing" is in the scientific age part of the development of chemical means of manipulation of the soil. The history of the geological impact of humans is also about the isolation of ingredients such as phosphorus (1669), nitrogen (1772), and potassium (1807). The years constitute recent events in the nonlinear history of earth becoming adapted to technical cultural history. The technical-scientific ties with together with the anthrobscene too: "The arrival of industrialization, ushering in the Anthropocene, is marked by the human ability to move vast quantities of geologic material."[27]

Nation-states and their media-supported wars are themselves fueled by material explorations and, to put it simply, energy. But these are wars with a punctuated imbalance: as Sean Cubitt notes, much of the contemporary geological resource hunt and energy race is conditioned by neocolonial arrangements, targeting territories traditionally belonging to indigenous people: "Geological resources are sourced in lands previously deemed worthless and therefore earmarked as reservations for displaced indigenous peoples during the period of European imperial expansion from the eighteenth to the twentieth centuries."[28] This is a good way of demonstrating that in some ways contemporary states—and corporations—are still utterly modern in their manner of operations. Eviction, massacre, and conquering are part of the normal repository of actions allowed in guaranteeing resources, as Geoffrey Winthrop-Young writes.[29]

Oil is the usual reference point for a critical evaluation of earth fossils, modern technological culture, and the link between nation-state and corporate interests in exploiting cheap labor and cheap resources. But of course it is not the only one. Other material is also moved on an increasingly massive scale and with an important function in the militarily secured energy regimes of the globe. Genealogies of logistics, media, and warfare are particularly "Kittlerian"; what is missing from his media materialism is often the theme of labor. Indeed, we could as justifiably track down genealogies of media materials back to labor processes, exploitation, and the dangerous conditions that characterize also the current persistence of *hardwork* alongside persistence of *hardware*. [30] Perhaps these two are better indexes of digital culture than software creativity or immaterial labor.

Notes

1. Sean Cubitt, Robert Hassan, and Ingrid Volkmer, "Does Cloud Computing Have a Silver Lining?" *Media, Culture & Society* 33 (2011): 149–58.

2. Paul Feigelfeld, "From the Anthropocene to the Neo-Cybernetic Underground: A Conversation with Erich Hörl," *Modern Weekly*, Fall/Winter 2013, online English version at http://www.60pages.com/from-the-anthropocene-to-the-neo-cybernetic-underground-a-conversation-with-erich-horl-2/.

3. Ibid.

4. Bratton, *The Stack*. Michael Nest, *Coltan*.

5. Rob Holmes, "A Preliminary Atlas of Gizmo Landscapes," *Mammolith*,

April 1, 2010, http://m.ammoth.us/blog/2010/04/a-preliminary-atlas-of-gizmo-landscapes/.

6. Jay Goldberg, "Hardware Is Dead," *Venturebeat*, September 15, 2012, http://venturebeat.com/2012/09/15/hardware-is-dead/.

7. Bruce Sterling, "The Dead Media Project: A Modest Proposal and a Public Appeal," http://www.deadmedia.org/modest-proposal.html.

8. Goldberg, "Hardware Is Dead."

9. Ibid.

10. For a specific focus on scrap metals, technology, and China, see Adam Minter, "How China Profits from Our Junk," *The Atlantic*, November 1, 2013, www.theatlantic.com/. On the life cycle of metals as part of technological society, see Graedel et al., "On the Materials Basis of Modern Society," 1–6.

11. Ibid.

12. Garnet Hertz and Jussi Parikka, "Zombie Media: Circuit Bending Media Archaeology into an Art Method," *Leonardo* 45, no. 5 (2012): 424–30.

13. U.S. Environmental Protection Agency, "Statistics on the Management of Used and End-of-Life Electronics," 2009, http://www.epa.gov/osw/conserve/materials/ecycling/manage.htm.

14. McKenzie Wark, "Escape from the Dual Empire," *Rhizomes* 6 (Spring 2003), http://www.rhizomes.net/issue6/wark.htm.

15. Michael T. Klare, *The Race for What's Left: The Global Scramble for the World's Last Resources* (New York: Metropolitan Books, 2012), 12.

16. "Chevron Announces Discovery in the Deepest Well Drilled in the U.S. Gulf of Mexico," press release, December 20, 2005, http://investor.chevron.com/.

17. Martin Heidegger, *The Question Concerning Technology and Other Essays*, trans. William Lovitt (New York: Garland Publishing, 1977), 16.

18. European Union Critical Raw Materials Analysis, by the European Commission Raw Materials Supply Group, July 30, 2010, executive summary by Swiss Metal Assets, October 1, 2011. www.swissmetalassets.com.

19. Clemens Winkler, "Germanium, Ge, ein neues, nichtmetallisches Element," *Berichte der deutschen chemischen Gesellschaft* 19 (1886): 210–11

20.   See Ryan Bishop, "Project 'Transparent Earth,'"

21.   Rosalind Williams, *Notes on the Underground: An Essay on Technology, Society, and the Imagination,* new ed. (Cambridge, Mass.: The MIT Press, 2008).

22.   The underground was also the home of technological magic much earlier than this, such as Celtic "people under the hill" who had marvelous objects at their command, or Teutonic dwarves who were the masters of metal and invention, including the Kobolds, for whom cobalt was named.

23.   McKenzie Wark, *Telesthesia: Communication, Culture & Class* (Cambridge: Polity, 2012), 12.

24.   Jonathan Sterne has also flagged the need for a deep time perspective, without using those terms: "if the span of media history in human history amounts to approximately 40,000 years, we have yet to really seriously reconsider the first 39,400 years." Jonathan Sterne, "The Times of Communication History," presented at Connections: The Future of Media Studies, University of Virginia, April 4, 2009.

25.   Friedrich Kittler, "Of States and Their Terrorists," *Cultural Politics* 8, no. 3 (2012): 388. See also the University of Brighton project "Traces of Nitrate: Mining History and Photography between Britain and Chile," funded by the AHRC. Online at http://arts.brighton.ac.uk/projects/traces-of-nitrate.

26.   Ibid., 394.

27.   Chris Taylor, "Fertilising Earthworks," in *Making the Geologic Now: Responses to the Material Conditions of Contemporary Life,* ed. Elizabeth Ellsworth and Jamie Kruse (New York: Punctum, 2013), 130.

28.   Sean Cubitt, "Integral Waste," presentation at the transmediale 2014 Afterglow-festival, Berlin, February 1, 2014. The paper is forthcoming in published form in the journal *Theory, Culture & Society*.

29.   Geoffrey Winthrop-Young, "Hunting a Whale of a State: Kittler and His Terrorists," *Cultural Politics* 8, no. 3 (2012): 406. He continues with a reference to Pynchon's words about World War II in *Gravity's Rainbow* (1973) but perhaps a relevant guideline to the wider issue of media, materiality, ideology and wars: "This War was never political at all, the politics was all theatre, all just to keep the people distracted . . . secretly, it was being dictated instead by the needs of technology. . . .The real crises were crises of allocation and priority, not among firms—it was

only staged to look that way—but among the different Technologies, Plastics, Electronics, Aircraft, and their needs which are understood only by the ruling elite." Quoted in Winthrop-Young, 407.

30.   *iMine* game, http://i-mine.org/. See also Parikka, "Dust and Exhaustion."

4

Conclusion: Cultural Techniques of Material Media

In Thomas Pynchon's *Against the Day*, a novel set before the digital era and more focused on the modulation and standardization of processes of light for the use of technical media such as photography, one gets a sense of the chemistry of media. Pynchon's status as part of theoretical mapping of history of media and technology has become consolidated ever since *Gravity's Rainbow* (1973) tied together war, technology, and a weird narrative mix of paranoia, conspiracy, and mental states. The V-2 rocket motivated insights into technology and science as an essential part of power relations inspired by the likes of Kittler but also a range of later scholars. In *Against the Day* (2006) the theme is similar but with a focus on light, optics, and chemistry, where especially the latter is what connects to our need to understand media history to its materials. It is an account that persists from the early histories of photography such as geologist-photographer W. Jerome Harrison's *History of Photography* (1887), which if you read it through the perspective of geology of media becomes a story of chemicals instead of merely the inventor-experimenters such as Niepce, Daguerre, or Talbot: bitumen (in lithography), tin, iodide, lactates and nitrates of silver, carbon processes, uranium nitrates, and chlorides of gold.[1] History of technical media is constantly being reenacted in different ways in contemporary media arts. For photochemical artists getting their hands dirty with gelatin and silver nitrates this is part of the artistic methodology infused in chemistry: cyanotypes' esthetic effect comes down to chemicals (ammonium iron (III) citrate and potassium ferricyanide). A film artist with a media archaeological bent knows the amounts in combinations needed in testing and experimenting with chemicals/materials.[2] But this knowledge is more that of a metallurgist than of a scientist: experimentations in dosage, learning the materials' characteristics by practice.[3]

In Pynchon's own version of media materialism and optical media the list of objects constitutes a sort of a pre-mediatic media materialism, a list of voluntary or involuntary participants in the process of technical imaging, circa nineteenth century:

> After going through all the possible silver compounds, Merle moved on to salts of gold, platinum, copper, nickel, uranium, molybdenum, and antimony, abandoning metallic compounds after a while for resins, squashed bugs, coal-tar dyes, cigar smokes, wildflower extracts, urine from various critters including himself, reinvesting what little money came in from portrait work into lenses, filters, glass plates, enlarging machines, so that soon the wagon was just a damn rolling photography lab.[4]

Besides the object world with which the narrative continues—the world an object-oriented theorist might call "flat,"[5] which includes a litany from humans to lampposts to trolley dynamos and flush toilets—much has already happened on the level of chemical reactions. In other words, the media devices are not the only aspects of "materialism." We are, however, interested in questions of what enables and sustains media to become media.

In this sort of perspective on deep-time geologies as well as chemistry of media one cannot avoid at least a brief mention of the long history of alchemy. Isn't it exactly the lineage of alchemy that is of relevance here? It has meant attributing a special force to the natural elements and their mixes, from base to precious: from realgar, sulfur, white arsenic, cinnabar, and especially mercury to gold, lead, copper, silver, and iron.[6] The history of alchemy is steeped in poetic narratives that present their own versions of deep times (for instance in pre-Christian Chinese alchemy);[7] The discipline occupies a position between arts and sciences.[8] In a way, as Newman notes, alchemy prepared the experimental way for much of later technological culture. There were many such developers: Avicenna with his *De congelatione* (at one point mistaken for a writing by Aristotle), and scholastic writers such as Vincent of Beauvais, Albertus Magnus, and Roger Bacon are examples of early thirteenth-century practitioners. In Vincent's *Speculum doctrinale,* written between 1244 and 1250, one gets a sense of alchemy as a "science of minerals," a practice-based excavation of their transmutational qualities. In Vincent's words alchemy "is properly the art of transmuting mineral bodies, such as metals and the like, from their own species to others."[9]

In *Against the Day* Pynchon presents his own condensed narrative prose lineage from alchemy to modern chemistry and technical media. According to his way of crystallizing the chemistry of technological culture, this transformation of materials in knowledge and practices corresponds to the birth of capitalism, which is characterized by a regularization of processes of material reaction and metamorphosis. In *Against the Day* a dialogue between two characters, Merle and Webb, reveals something important about this turning point from alchemy to modern science:

"But if you look at the history, modern chemistry only starts coming in to replace alchemy around the same time capitalism really gets going. Strange, eh? What do you make of that?"

Webb nodded agreeably. "Maybe capitalism decided it didn't need the old magic anymore." An emphasis whose contempt was not meant to escape Merle's attention. "Why bother? Had their own magic, doin just fine, thanks, instead of turning lead into gold, they could take poor people's sweat and turn it into greenbacks, and save that lead for enforcement purposes."[10]

What Pynchon brings into play in this admittedly short quote is labor. Such issues link up with histories of exploitation and capture of surplus value, as well as with media histories of matter. Indeed, besides writing a material history of media before it becomes media, Pynchon is able to highlight the magical nature of commodity production related to the novel forms of "alchemy": the new magic explicated by Marx as the fetish of the object hiding the material forces of its production is characteristic of this aspect, which is usually defined as material history understood as a history of labor and political economy. We need to also understand, however, the technological and media elements in this mix, which also returns to the issue of geology, the earth.

In short, techniques of experimenting with different reactions and combinations are also media practices. Our screen technologies, cables, networks, technical means of seeing and hearing, are partly results of meticulous—and sometimes just purely accidental—experimentation with how materials work; what works, what doesn't, whether you are talking about materials for insulation, conduction, projection, or recording. The sciences and the arts often share this attitude of experimentation and the experiment—to make the *geos* expressive and transformative. The transistor-based information tech culture would not be thinkable without the various meticulous insights into the material characteristics and differences between germanium and silicon—or the energetic regimes; whether that involves the consideration of current clouds (as in server farms), or the attempts to manage power consumption inside computer architectures.[11] Issues of energy are ones of geophysics too—both in the sense of climate change accelerated by the still continuing heavy reliance on polluting forms of nonrenewable energy production and through the various chemicals, metals, and metalloids such as germanium and silicon, media cultural aftereffects of the geological strata. That is also where a deep time of the planet is inside our machines, crystallized as part of the contemporary political economy: material histories of labor and the planet are entangled in devices, which however unfold as part of planetary histories. Data mining might be a leading hype term for our digital age of the moment but it is enabled only by the sort of mining that we associate with the ground and its ungrounding. Digital culture starts in the depths and deep times of the planet. Sadly, this story is most often more obscene than something to be celebrated with awe.

Notes

1. William Jerome Harrison, *History of Photography* (New York: Scovill Manufacturing Company, 1887). What makes Harrison even more interesting for our purposes is his career in geology. See Adam Bobbette, "Episodes from the History of Scalelessness: William Jerome Harrison and Geological Photography," in *Architecture in the Anthropocene: Encounters among Design, Deep Time, Science, and Philosophy*, 45–58.

2. Thank you to Kelly Egan for sharing the autoethnographic account of her artistic practice with films and chemicals.

3. Jane Bennett uses this conceptual figure, borrowed from Deleuze and Guattari, as well. See Jane Bennett, *Vibrant Matter: A Political Ecology of Things* (Durham, N.C.: Duke University Press, 2009), 58–60.

4. Thomas Pynchon, *Against the Day* (London: Vintage Books, 2007), 72.

5. See Paul Caplan, "JPEG: The Quadruple Object," (PhD thesis, Birkbeck College, University of London, 2013).

6. Homer H. Dubs, "The Beginnings of Alchemy," *Isis* 38, no. 1/2 (November 1947): 73.

7. "When the effluvia from the cow lands ascend to the dark heavens, the dark heavens in six hundred years' give birth to black whetstones, black whetstones in six hundred years give birth to black quicksilver, black quicksilver in six hundred years gives birth to black metal (iron), and black metal in a thousand years gives birth to a black dragon. Where the black dragon enters into [permanent] hibernation, it gives birth to the Black Springs," quoted in Dubs, "Alchemy," 72–73.

8. William Newman, "Technology and Alchemic Debate in the Late Middle Ages," *Isis* 80, no. 3 (September 1989): 426.

9. Vincent of Beauvais's *Speculum doctrinale,* quoted in Newman, "Technology and Alchemic Debate," 430.

10. Pynchon, *Against the Day*, 88.

11. Sean Cubitt, Robert Hassan, and Ingrid Volkmer, "Does Cloud Computing Have a Silver Lining?" See also Michael Riordan and Lillian Hoddeson, *Crystal Fire: The Invention of the Transistor and the Birth of the Information Age* (New York: W. W. Norton, 1997).

Acknowledgments

I owe thanks to several people who commented or otherwise helped to formulate my argument, including Shannon Mattern, Ryan Bishop, Benjamin Bratton, Sean Cubitt, Seb Franklin, Jonathan Kemp, Kelly Egan, and many others. I also thank Danielle Kasprzak and her colleagues at the University of Minnesota Press.

Earlier versions of this text were presented at University of Bochum, Goldsmiths (London), Cornell University, and Slade School of Fine Art at University College London. Thanks to Winchester School of Art for granting me the time necessary to work on *The Anthrobscene* and its follow-up volume, *A Geology of Media.*

Jussi Parikka is professor in technological culture and aesthetics at Winchester School of Art, University of Southampton and docent in digital culture theory at University of Turku. He is author of *What Is Media Archaeology?*; *Insect Media: An Archaeology of Animals and Technology* (Minnesota, 2010); and *Digital Contagions: A Media Archaeology of Computer Viruses.*